IMAGINE

IMAGINE

God Can Do More Than You Ever Dreamed

Margaret Feinberg

Foreword by Sheila Walsh

THOMAS NELSON
Since 1798

NASHVILLE   DALLAS   MEXICO CITY   RIO DE JANEIRO

Published in Nashville, Tennessee, by Thomas Nelson. Thomas Nelson is a trademark of Thomas Nelson, Inc.

Thomas Nelson, Inc., titles may be purchased in bulk for educational, business, fund-raising, or sales promotional use. For information, please e-mail SpecialMarkets@ThomasNelson.com.

ISBN: 978-1-4185-4186-6

Printed in China

10 11 12 13 14 RRD 6 5 4 3 2

Contents

Foreword   vii

Introduction: All in a Mind's Eye   ix

Reigniting Your Imagination

1   Embrace Your Imagination   3

2   The Beauty of Story   11

3   The Wonder of God   17

God Wants to Use You

4   Putting Yourself in Someone Else's Shoes   25

5   Aware of the Needs   31

6   Unexpectedly Used by God   37

Sprouting New Faith

7   Growing in Faith   47

8   Tapping into His Power   53

9   Stories of Great Faith   61

Contents

Conquering the Impossible

10 Nothing Is Impossible for God 69

11 Believing in the Impossible 75

12 Called to the Impossible 81

Leader's Guide 89

Notes 111

About the Author 113

Foreword

As a child I was frequently told that I had a vivid imagination. I was never quite sure if the observation was meant kindly or as a criticism. If it was said with a smile then I felt accepted as I was. But if it was passed on with a gentle shake of the head, I had the sneaky suspicion that disapproval was tucked in there somewhere. As life moved on I learned to imagine less and accept "what is" more, but some dreams are hard to suppress.

I grew up in Scotland, a culture that frowns upon getting ideas above one's station in life. I remember having a conversation with a teacher when I was in high school. He wanted to know what career I was considering pursuing when I graduated. I tried to gauge from his eyes how open he was to the life I really imagined and decided to share my dream anyway. I told him that I imagined spending the rest of my life telling people about the love of God. I imagined going into prisons and schools, college campuses and churches and letting people know that the God of the universe is crazy about them. He held my gaze for a moment and then he laughed. It wasn't a sweet, "wow" kind of laugh. It was a laugh of derision, and I knew in that moment that the story would be passed around the teachers' lounge later that day.

I don't blame my teacher for his outburst, for dreams outside the sovereignty and grace of God can seem impossible. But the truth is, I have spent my life telling people about the love of God. I have wept with women in prisons who will not hold their children for years to come. I have shared my story in schools, colleges, and churches around the world. What I have learned on my journey is something that makes a good bumper sticker but is harder to grasp hold of in our hearts—*With God, Nothing Is Impossible.*

One of my favorite verses from the Psalms is "Delight yourself also in the LORD, and He shall give you the desires of your heart" (37:4 NKJV). As a child I thought this meant that whatever I wanted, God would be glad to give me, be it a pony or a playmate. Now I understand that, as I delight myself in the Lord, He will anoint my imagination and give me His dreams to dream. The more I press in to know Him, the clearer my vision and imagination become.

As you look at your life right now, it may seem as if there is no room for imagination or you are too old for such silly stuff. There is quite a difference, however, between fantasy and imagination. Fantasy is the stuff of soap operas and made-for-TV movies, but God gave you an imagination so that you could join your heart with His and just see what He might do with and through you—just imagine that!

—SHEILA WALSH

Introduction

All in a Mind's Eye

God has given you so much. He's given you wisdom, grace, and beauty. He's given you family and friends. He has blessed you with tenacity and strength. Yet one of the most powerful gifts God has given you is imagination.

Have you ever considered what your life would be like without imagination? Without the ability to imagine, it would be impossible to dream. Without the ability to imagine, it would be difficult to hope. Without the ability to imagine, we couldn't create. Imagination is one of the greatest gifts that God has given us, and it's important to celebrate this gift by using it every chance we get.

Do you know who some of the most imaginative people on the planet are? Children. Kids have a knack for using their imaginations. In the eyes of a child, a couch is easily transformed into a huge Viking ship; a queen-sized sheet, draped over furniture, becomes a fortress; and a plastic doll is a living, breathing baby who needs to be held. Yet, somewhere along the road to adulthood, we lose grasp of our natural ability to imagine. We stop seeing the Viking ships or taking time to play "house." Where did our wild, colorful, and beautiful imaginations go?

In a world created by our unlimited God, why do we allow our imaginations to become stifled as we grow older? The truth is your imagination is too good a gift to tuck away for one more day. My hope and prayer is that you will rediscover your childlike ability to imagine as you go through this study. Along the way, may the expectation and excitement of what God wants to do in and through you be unleashed. God has big plans for you—bigger than you can ever imagine.

Blessings,
Margaret Feinberg

Reigniting Your Imagination

All of us are given imaginations; how much do we use them? This section is designed to help you recapture your ability to imagine new possibilities in your life and journey with God.

One

Embrace Your Imagination

*Do not quench your inspiration
and your imagination.*

VINCENT VAN GOGH

Do you remember when, as a child, you were able to transform a box of old clothes into a wardrobe fit for a royal family? Did you ever build forts and caves in the living room with an old quilt? Did you ever play games with friends pretending to be a teacher, a princess, or even a pilot? As children, all the wonderful places our imaginations took us were amazing. We explored new worlds, discovered buried treasure, and delighted in imaginary meals.

All too often, imagination fades or ceases to be a priority as we grow older. Settling into professions, raising families, and paying mortgages all have a way of distracting us from our sense of awe and wonder. How imaginative are you today? To get a glimpse, take the following quiz:

Embrace Your Imagination

1. Which type of books do you prefer to read?

   A. Nonfiction.
   B. Adventure and fantasy.
   C. A good mix of both.

2. Which is your favorite color group?

   A. Black, white, and neutral tones.
   B. Bright red, green, yellow, and blue.
   C. A blend of colors and neutrals.

3. When you tell a story, do you:

   A. Tell the facts and just the facts?
   B. Make the story sound larger-than-life?
   C. Tell the story with enough detail to keep people listening?

4. When you look at clouds in the sky, do you see specific images (like faces or animals)?

   A. Never.
   B. All the time.
   C. Sometimes.

5. How would you respond if a child woke you complaining about monsters under the bed?

   A. Gently tell the child it was a bad dream and urge them back to bed.
   B. Spray monster repellent over and under the bed.
   C. Comfort the child, reminding him or her that monsters don't exist; even if they did, God is still more powerful.

6. *How often do you have vivid dreams?*

   A. Zero to one time per week.

   B. Almost every night.

   C. Two to four times per week.

If you answered mostly As, you may have allowed your imagination to sit on the back burner too long; but it's never too late to re-ignite it! Go ahead and begin looking for opportunities to allow your imagination to simmer. Spend an afternoon looking at the clouds and search for fun images. Spend an evening playing games with a child. Look for opportunities to enter a child's (naturally creative) world. You'll be amazed how quickly your imagination comes to life.

Look for opportunities to enter a child's (naturally creative) world.

If you answered mostly Bs, you have a vibrant, colorful imagination. You can be a source of encouragement to others who want to remember how to dream and live creatively. In daily life, you'll need to be careful that your imagination doesn't get in the way of relationships or your ability to accomplish tasks and fulfill commitments.

If you answered mostly Cs, your imagination is bubbling steadily in your life. You still allow it to come to life and it colors how you see the world. Go out of your way during the upcoming weeks to nurture your imagination, sharing what you learn with others.

1. *Did you tend to answer mostly As, Bs, or Cs in the Embrace Your Imagination quiz?*

5

2. When you were a child, what were some ways you used your imagination? What specific games did you like to play that involved using your imagination?

3. Think about the past week. Were there any situations that required you to use your imagination? If so, describe.

In John 13–17, we find the account of Jesus' last meal with His disciples before His death. As they began their meal, Jesus announced that one of the disciples would betray Him. The news shocked everyone. They could hardly believe what Jesus was saying. Then Jesus told Peter he would go so far as to deny knowing Christ. Jesus' words troubled the disciples, but He comforted them.

4. Read John 14:1–14. How did Jesus comfort His followers?

The word *imagine* means "to form a mental image of something not actually present to the senses."[1]

5. Do you think the disciples tried to imagine the place Jesus was describing (vv. 2–3)? Why or why not?

6. How do you imagine the place Jesus was describing (vv. 2–3)?

7. How do you think Jesus' words in this passage comforted the disciples?

8. How does this passage comfort you?

The things God has in store for us are beyond our wildest imaginations.

Digging Deeper

Read **Revelation 21:22–27**. What does this passage reveal about heaven? What does this passage reveal about God's love for us? What are your expectations of heaven?

Bonus Activity

Take a simple household object (like a paper bag, a vase, or a telephone) and pass it among members of your group. Challenge each person to imagine a use for the object different from the one for which it was intended. A paper bag might become a mask or a piece of luggage; a vase might become a change collector or a hat; a telephone might become a pendant or a level. Be creative. Have fun. Don't forget to laugh!

Two

The Beauty of Story

*Even an old barn looks better
with a fresh coat of paint.*

<small>UNKNOWN</small>

What is your favorite children's story? Did you enjoy *The Giving Tree* by Shel Silverstein or *Heidi* by Johanna Spyri? Did you find delight in *Goodnight Moon* by Margaret Wise Brown or *Green Eggs and Ham* by Dr. Seuss? Or are you more a fan of *Charlotte's Web* by E. B. White or *Charlie and the Chocolate Factory* by Roald Dahl?

Stories have a way of communicating truth in powerful and compelling ways. We may remember something we are told directly; but when that same information is given through story, it tends to stick with us in a more permanent way. A great story can change the way we think, act, and even the way we respond to others. Stories engage our imaginations and teach us lessons about ourselves, our world, and even our faith. Jesus regularly used stories to illustrate deep truths about God. Even in our modern world, we still use stories to teach lessons, provide insights, and capture people's hearts and imaginations.

Consider the following story: *A great storm stranded a monkey on a deserted island. The small creature found a sheltered place on the land where he could wait for the storm to pass and the raging waters to calm. The monkey soon noticed fish swimming in the rough, storm-tossed sea near the island. They seemed to be struggling and in need of help. Being a kind monkey, he decided to help the fish. He found a tree limb that reached out above the seemingly troubled fish. Putting himself in great peril, he climbed out on the limb, reached down into the water, and scooped the fish out of the turbulent sea. He quickly returned to the place of his shelter and laid the fish on dry ground. For a few brief moments, the fish seemed excited; then they settled into a peaceful rest.*

When we don't take the time to find out the real needs of others but rather serve them only on the basis of our own opinions (or worse, what makes us feel good), we can do more damage than good.

We are sometimes tempted to get involved in a situation without fully understanding all the details or the best way to make a positive difference in the lives of those involved. When we don't take the time to find out the real needs of others but rather serve them only on the basis of our own opinions (or worse, what makes us feel good), we can do more damage than good. This story catches the reader by surprise; it seems the monkey is doing good when he's really doing harm. The fish cannot survive on dry land.

Like this tale of the fish and the monkey, some stories make powerful points but do so subtly; others rely on gross exaggerations and silly comparisons. Still others use humor and puns. All these elements have a way of igniting our imaginations and helping us experience an idea, thought, or lesson from a different perspective.

1. *What are some of your favorite children's stories?*

   Heidi

   Elsie Dinsmore

   Bible Stories

2. *What are some common characteristics shared by your favorite children's stories?*

3. *How do these common children's book characteristics differ from the characteristics of your book choices as an adult? What characteristics are the same?*

4. Reread the story of the monkey and fish. What life lessons can you draw from this story?

5. Have you ever felt like the monkey in a life situation? The fish? Describe.

Jesus often used stories or parables to engage people's minds, hearts, and imaginations. The word *parable* comes from the Greek term *parabole*. The word describes a story that creates a stark contrast or illustration for the listener. Some parables simply use word pictures—images painted with words—while others use more complex analogy.

One of Jesus' parables relayed an important message directed toward religious leaders of the time.

6. Read *Matthew 21:28–32*. What is the stark contrast between the two sons?

7. Who did Jesus suggest the first son was like? Who did Jesus suggest the second son was like?

8. What elements of this story were probably shocking to the listeners? In your own spiritual life, to which of the two sons do you most easily relate? Why?

Stories are powerful tools for teaching spiritual lessons and illustrating truths. They invoke our imaginations and cause us to think differently.

Digging Deeper

Jesus used parables to describe profound truths about God and His kingdom. Read **Matthew 13:44–45**. What are the two things that represent the kingdom of heaven in this passage? What did the men do when they found the valuables? Why do you think they responded in this way to finding the treasures? How have you responded to God's presence in your life? What sacrifices have you made to grow in your relationship with God and know Him more? Has it been worth it? Why or why not?

Bonus Activity

Select one or two brief children's books that are popular today or were beloved during your childhood. Spend some time thinking about what makes each story so delightful. How do the stories engage your imagination? What valuable lessons do they teach?

Three

The Wonder of God

*It is not from ourselves that we learn
to be better than we are.*

WENDELL BERRY

Have you ever noticed how people sometimes use words or phrases that don't mean anything at all? Or they add words to their expressions that, like, well, you know, make it harder to understand what they're really saying?

Place a check mark by all the expressions below you've heard people use during the last week:

___ To tell you the truth	___ In a perfect world
___ Seriously	___ I, personally
___ The reality is	___ Fairly unique
___ Yeah, no	___ Really
___ Same old	___ You know what I mean
___ It's a no-brainer	___ It is what it is
___ For crying out loud	___ Seriously
___ Blah, blah, blah	___ Yada, yada
___ Um, okay	___ I hate to say it, but

— Cool

It's amazing how many phrases and words we use that have no real substance or have lost their meaning from overuse. For example, some people will call God "awesome," but they also use "awesome" to describe a triple cheeseburger, a sporty new car, or a Labrador puppy. While food, cars, and puppies are delightful in their own way, nothing is truly as awesome as our God. The one who fashioned the heavens and created our earth is beyond comprehension. His presence can't help but leave us in awe.

The one who fashioned the heavens and created our earth is beyond comprehension.

Each of us has the ability to rediscover the real wonder that comes with being a child of God. When we take time to examine God's character and learn who God is through Scripture, we can't help but stand in awe of His power, strength, wisdom, and grace. Even our imaginations will fail us when it comes to wrapping our minds around an infinite, all-powerful God.

1. Which words do you tend to overuse?

2. Which overused or empty words would you add to the list on page 17?

3. *Like the word* awesome, *what are some words that describe God, but are overly used in other contexts?*

4. *Are there any words you use solely to describe God?*

holy

Job was a godly man who went through an intense period of suffering and loss. He was stripped of almost everything but managed to hold on to his faith in God. In Job 32–37, Elihu, one of Job's friends, described some of the wonders of God.

5. *Read* **Job 37**. *Make a list in the space below of all the things mentioned in this passage that inspire wonder and awe of God.*

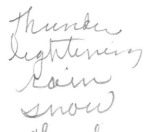

Thunder
lightening
rain
snow
clouds

sun

6. Which of these wonders is most wondrous to you?

7. Job 37:22 says, "God comes in awesome majesty." How often do you take time to reflect on the majesty of God?

8. How does knowing more about God and His infinite ways strengthen your own faith journey?

*God is almighty, powerful, and truly awesome.
Reflecting on the wonder of who God is and
all He has done strengthens our faith.*

Digging Deeper

Our imaginations can't even begin to grasp all that God is doing
in our lives. Read **Isaiah 55:8–9**. What is different between God's
thoughts and our thoughts? What is different between God's ways
and our ways? What comfort do you find in knowing God's ways are
so much different from yours?

Bonus Activity

When was the last time you used your creative mind to solve a
riddle? Consider the following two riddles. No. 1: A man went on a
trip on Friday, stayed for two days, and returned on Friday. How is
that possible? No. 2: An electric train is traveling south. The wind is
from the northwest. In which direction would the smoke from the
train be blowing? If you enjoyed these, consider checking out a book
of riddles from your local library and reviewing a handful before the
next session.

God Wants to Use You

God gave you an imagination, not just for

you to enjoy, but for you to use to bless others.

Whenever you choose to put yourself in someone

else's shoes or consider the possibilities of God's

will in someone else's life, you're using your

imagination. What a difference that can make!

Four

Putting Yourself in Someone Else's Shoes

Because how we spend our days is, of course, how we spend our lives.

ANNIE DILLARD

Picture the ultimate hippie: long, shaggy hair; tie-dyed T-shirt; ripped jeans; and no shoes. This description certainly fits one college student of the 1960s. This young man wasn't particularly outspoken, but he was a typical hippie-turned-Jesus-freak. He found Jesus while attending classes.

One Sunday, he decided to visit a conservative church. Everyone was wearing their Sunday best—dressed to impress. When this young man walked in with his colorful, tie-dyed T-shirt, bare feet, and earthy vibe, everyone was caught off guard. The young man was so focused on finding a place to sit he didn't even notice the raised eyebrows he was getting from those in the pews. Unable to find an empty spot in a pew, he finally gave up and innocently took a seat— right on the floor in the center of the front aisle.

No one knew what to do about this strange visitor. The tension in the room was unmistakable. Even the minister was caught off guard by the sight of the man sitting in the middle of the aisle. Everyone sat in silence. Finally, an elderly church deacon walked forward and slowly approached the young man. Most of the congregation expected the young man to be reprimanded for his lack of respect. Yet, after the deacon made his way down the aisle to where the man sat, he plopped down next to him and they began to worship God together. The entire congregation gasped in disbelief. The minister told the congregation that even though they probably wouldn't remember what he taught that Sunday morning, they should never forget the stunning example of the elderly deacon and the hippie seated on the floor and worshipping together.

As we use our imaginations and step out in faith to embrace those who are different, not only do we have an opportunity to grow in our own faith journeys, but we can also help others grow.

In each of our lives, there will be times we find ourselves in the role of the hippie and others when we play the part of the deacon. At times, we'll be the one who feels out of place—not sure exactly where we fit in and forced to make the best of the situation. At other times, we'll feel more like the deacon; we'll be the one with an opportunity to risk and include someone, making them feel comfortable even when those around us aren't so sure of our decision. In the end, love conquers all. As we use our imaginations and step out in faith to embrace those who are different, not only do we have an opportunity to grow in our own faith journeys, but we can also help others grow. We can bring peace-filled resolution to uncomfortable situations.

1. *Imagine if the deacon had never made the journey down the aisle. How do you think the outcome of the young man's visit to the church would have been affected?*

He would not have felt Welcome and my not have continued as a Christian

2. *How do you think you would have responded had you been in that church that Sunday morning? Explain.*

Just like the congregation - We would have felt he Wasn't dressed properly and was disrespectful

The hippie - culture was labeled - drug user, low class - drop outs - un patriotic - draft dodgers.

27

3. *The hippie visitor was a shock to a conservative church in the 1960s. What kind of person would be shocking to your faith community? A man in a prison uniform with a guard? Someone who had not bathed for two weeks? Other?*

4. *What's your immediate reaction to these types of people and situations?*

Better now - We have seen what the "Jesus" Movement did for them - We realize we were very judgmental

One widowed woman, Ruth, found herself an outcast in a city. She moved to Bethlehem with her widowed mother-in-law, Naomi. Their transition took place during a famine, and the women didn't even have food to sustain themselves. Ruth survived by gleaning; she followed behind the harvesters of the fields and gathered the leftovers from the crop.

5. Read **Ruth 1**. Do you think Naomi and Ruth ever imagined their lives would turn out as they did? Why or why not (Ruth 1:3–5)?

No. not while their husbands lived.

6. Read **Ruth 2**. How do you think Boaz imagined Ruth's life to be?

Very poor and needy.

7. What did Boaz do for Ruth (vv. 8–16)? Why did he do it (v. 11)?

Told her to gather only in his fields where she would be safe.

Because of her love and respect for Naomi.

8. *Why is it important to use our imaginations to put ourselves in other people's shoes? What helps you become more compassionate toward others?*

So we can understand what they are dealing with. Inquiring about them so we can know them better and not be judgmental

> *We can use our imaginations to put ourselves in other people's shoes and develop compassion for them.*

Digging Deeper

Boaz went beyond providing the bare minimum for Naomi and Ruth. Read **Ruth 4:1–12**. According to this passage, how did Boaz show compassion? How do you think Naomi and Ruth responded?

Bonus Activity

Visit a fast-food restaurant and purchase a few gift cards for simple meals. Carry the cards around in your car with you. The next time you see a homeless person or someone in need, give them a card so they can enjoy a hot meal.

July 25

Five

Aware of the Needs

The best exercise for strengthening the heart
is reaching down and lifting people up.

ERNEST BLEVINS

A few years ago, my husband, Leif, noticed a young boy at church whose shoes were falling apart. He knew the family, and though everything seemed to be fine, he felt compelled to ask the father if he could buy the son some new shoes. The father's eyes lit up. The family had wanted to buy their son new shoes for the upcoming basketball season but had recently experienced some financial set-backs. With the parents' permission, Leif took the boy to the shoe store and the boy picked out the pair he really wanted. Both Leif and the boy went home with big smiles on their faces.

Within our daily routines, we often cross paths with people who have specific needs. Yet, if we're not careful, we can easily miss them. We must have eyes to see the needs around us and hearts that are responsive to how God may want to use us to bless others.

Sometimes we have to be creative and imaginative as we think up ways to respond to these needs. Consider the following scenarios:

Scenario A: After volunteering at an event, you decide to join a group of the volunteers who are going out for lunch. As everyone is ordering, you notice the young lady beside you orders only a glass of water with lemon. You gently ask her if she's hungry and she says she ate earlier. You have a hunch that she just doesn't have the funds to pay for a meal. How do you respond?

We need to prayerfully consider how God wants to use us to meet the needs of others.

Scenario B: You discover a neighbor has just lost his job and received no severance package. He and his wife are concerned about providing for their three children. How do you respond?

Scenario C: You notice the pastor of your local church is looking really run-down lately. While he still faithfully serves the church each week, he has bags under his eyes and an unmistakable weight on his shoulders. You can't help but think he needs a pick-me-up. How do you respond?

When we encounter situations like these, we need to prayerfully consider how God wants to use us to meet the needs of others. We just may find that God gives us unique, out-of-the-box ideas to help make a difference.

1. *What are some practical, loving ways you could respond to scenarios A, B, and C?*

2. Have you ever encountered a situation like one of these scenarios? How did you respond?

3. Have you ever experienced being the person in need in a scenario similar to one of these? During that time, in what ways did people respond to you that were the most meaningful?

Being from Rome, the apostle Paul wanted to deliver the message of Jesus to his hometown, but many things got in the way. When Paul finally began the journey to Rome (as recorded in Acts 27–28), his boat encountered a dangerous storm.

4. Read *Acts 27:1–28:16*. What news did the angel of God give Paul *(Acts 27:24)*?

5. How did the islanders show compassion to those who were shipwrecked *(Acts 28:2, 7, 10)*?

The compassion that we experience and show to others is like a snapshot of the incredible love and care God has for each of us. Deuteronomy 10:17–18 says, "For the LORD your God is God of gods and Lord of lords, the great God, mighty and awesome, who shows no partiality and accepts no bribes. He defends the cause of the fatherless and the widow, and loves the alien, giving him food and clothing."

God defends the cause of the poor, weak, and marginalized and He calls us to do the same. In Matthew 25, Jesus offered a profound reminder: when we care for the least it's as if we're caring for Him.

6. Read **Matthew 25:31–46**. *According to this parable, what are the defining characteristics of a sheep? A goat?*

7. *Do you think it's easier to be a sheep or a goat? Why? Like which are you most tempted to behave?*

8. *Do you know anyone who is "hungry or thirsty or a stranger or needing clothes or sick or in prison" (Matthew 25:44)? What opportunities do you have as an individual (and as a group) to care for others as if they were Christ?*

God calls us to meet the needs of others. Sometimes serving others and making a difference will involve finding creative solutions and using our imaginations to help solve problems.

Digging Deeper

Paul and his friend Silas were caught in a sticky situation. Read **Acts 16:16–34.** How did Paul and Silas end up in prison? What were Paul and Silas doing when the earthquake struck? How did Paul and Silas show compassion for the jailer? How did the jailer show compassion for Paul and Silas? Have you ever shown compassion to someone in need? How did it turn out?

Bonus Activity

Go to your local pastor or visit a local nonprofit and ask if there are any specific needs within your community your group can meet. If no opportunities are immediately available, ask them to keep your group in mind as a source of help when a situation of need becomes known.

Six

Unexpectedly Used by God

Knowing that I am not the one in control
gives great encouragement. Knowing the
One who is in control is everything.

ALEXANDER MICHAEL

In his book *God's Smuggler*, Brother Andrew shares the amazing adventures he experienced while taking Bibles into the Soviet Union and Europe years before the fall of the Iron Curtain. On one particular trip to Romania, Brother Andrew experienced a rather harrowing situation. He was seventh in a line of cars waiting to pass through the border patrol into Romania. Rather than offer a quick inspection or simply wave the drivers through, the officers were actually taking the vehicles apart—dismantling the seats, removing hubcaps, and even disassembling engines. The officers were on a mission to find the tiniest bit of contraband, which included religious literature.

Brother Andrew was next in line for inspection and he prayed a rather unusual prayer. Reasoning that there was no way he could hide all the Bibles in the back of his vehicle, he asked God to allow him to leave the Bibles in the open where the officers would see them. That way, he figured, he'd be totally dependent on God. Rather than try to outwit the guards, Brother Andrew took several Bibles from the back of his vehicle and placed them on the front seat beside him. A guard waved him forward to the inspection point. Brother Andrew started to open his car door for the inspection, but the guard held his leg against it, pinning the door closed. He examined Brother Andrew's passport, wrote something down, handed back the papers, and waved Brother Andrew on. The whole incident took only thirty seconds. Had the guard seen the Bibles? Was he supposed to pull over for a more thorough inspection? Looking into his rearview mirror, Brother Andrew watched as the guard approached the next car. The driver was forced to step out of the car for a full inspection. Brother Andrew realized he had been spared the inspection and was free to go.

> *Though there is always a place for planning and strategizing, there are times when God will invite us to trust Him for the miraculous.*

This incident was only one of many in which Brother Andrew found himself abandoning his own strategies and choosing to depend fully on God. Though there is always a place for planning and strategizing, there are times when God will invite us to trust Him for the miraculous. In those moments, it's amazing to see God at work.

While the way we serve God with our lives may not be as dramatic as Brother Lawrence's smuggling Bibles behind the Iron Curtain, we each have daily opportunities to share our faith, encourage others, and reach out to those who need us. Often, we'll need to ask God to get us through. When we put our faith in Him, there's just no telling what God might do. It may truly be beyond anything we could ever expect or imagine!

1. *How do you think you would have responded to the situation if you were Brother Andrew?*

I would have been scared but prayed also.

2. *Have you ever found yourself in a sticky situation and really needed God to get you through? Describe.*

3. *What kinds of everyday situations cause the most growth in your faith? Do you tend to embrace these situations or try to avoid them? Why?*

I seem to pray about everything - Especially when my kids have situations

Moses was a man who found himself unexpectedly used by God. Though Jewish by birth, Moses grew up in Egypt and was raised by one of Pharaoh's daughters. After fleeing Egypt, Moses became a shepherd. While caring for the flocks of his father-in-law, Jethro, Moses had an unforgettable encounter with God.

4. Read **Exodus 3:1–14**. What does God ask of Moses? How would you have responded if you were in Moses' shoes? What is Moses' first concern with God's plan (v. 11)? What is Moses' second concern with God's plan (v. 13)? What is God's response to Moses' concerns?

Who am I to appear before Pharaoh

They won't believe me and ask Which God are you talking about

I am — the God of your ancestors

5. Read **Exodus 4:10–12**. What is Moses' concern about going to Egypt (v. 10)? What is God's response to Moses' concern (vv. 11–12)?

I can't talk, I get tongue tied

God said who made your mouth and tongue - I did now go and I will help you.

Moses chose to obey God and to return to Egypt. With the help of his brother, Aaron, he was to deliver God's message to Pharaoh. Pharaoh did not listen to or believe anything Moses and Aaron told him. As a result of Pharaoh's repeated refusal to let God's people leave, God sent a series of plagues on Egypt.

6. Fill in the chart below according to the Scripture listed.

Scripture Reference	Plague That Occurred
Exodus 7:19	flood
Exodus 8:6	frogs
Exodus 8:16	gnats
Exodus 8:21	flies
Exodus 9:3	death to livestock
Exodus 9:8–9	boils
Exodus 9:18	hail
Exodus 10:4–5	locust
Exodus 10:21–23	darkness
Exodus 11:4–5	death of first born

Reflecting on the list of plagues above, which would be the scariest to you? The grossest? The most disturbing?

After the final plague, Pharaoh's heart was finally softened and he agreed to let God's people go. Read **Exodus 12:29–32** aloud:

At midnight the Lord struck down all the firstborn in Egypt, from the firstborn of Pharaoh, who sat on the throne, to the firstborn of the prisoner, who was in the dungeon, and the firstborn of all the livestock as well. Pharaoh and all his officials and all the Egyptians got up during the night, and there was loud wailing in Egypt, for there was not a house without someone dead. During the night Pharaoh summoned Moses and Aaron and said, "Up! Leave my people, you and the Israelites! Go, worship the Lord as you have requested. Take your flocks and herds, as you have said, and go. And also bless me."

7. What made this last plague the worst of all the plagues for Pharaoh? Why do you think he finally agreed to let the Israelites leave Egypt?

Death of all first born

8. Why do you think Pharaoh asked Moses and Aaron to bless him (Exodus 12:32)? Why is this significant? Do you think Moses and Aaron were surprised by this response? Why or why not?

> No matter how unqualified or undeserving we may feel, God wants to use us. As He did with Moses, He may use us to set people free.

Digging Deeper

Before he became the Apostle to the Gentiles, Paul persecuted Christians. He tried to destroy the very belief system he later embraced. Read 2 Corinthians 12:7–10. What specific situations remind you that God's grace is sufficient for you? Repeat the phrase "my power is made perfect in weakness" (v. 9) in your own words. Do you find it difficult or easy to delight in weaknesses, insults, hardships, persecutions, and difficulties?

Bonus Activity

Create a decorative pencil. Select pieces of colorful paper. Consider using wrapping paper or decorative paper from a stationery store. Purchase a pack of unsharpened pencils and some Mod Podge or other type of hobby glue. Cut the paper one inch shorter than the length of the pencil you want to decorate. Spread the glue on the back of the paper and carefully roll the pencil along the paper until it's covered. Presto! You have a decorative pencil! Now, use the pencil to write a note of encouragement to someone you haven't spoken to in five years or more.

Sprouting
New Faith

As we imagine all that God desires

to do in our lives, our faith can't

help but grow. As we step out in

faith, we discover more about who

God is and all that He has for us.

Seven

Growing in Faith

When we have an atom of faith in our hearts, we
can see God's face, gentle, serene, and approving.

JOHN CALVIN

Thomas Jefferson, one of the men who helped draft the Declaration of Independence, believed Jesus was a good man with incredible principles, but he didn't quite believe all of the supernatural occurrences within the Gospels. Jefferson believed that the teachings of Christ had been muffled over the years by priests and teachers who preached about the miracles surrounding Jesus. Jefferson took matters into his own hands when he decided to delete every mention of a miracle in Scripture, including the virgin birth and the resurrection. He extracted select verses from the four Gospels, rearranged them in chronological order, and created a single narrative, leaving out all mention of prophecy, angels, or the Trinity. His own unique version of Scripture became known as the Jefferson Bible.

For Thomas Jefferson, Jesus was not the Messiah or Son of God; Jefferson believed He was merely a moral teacher. The Jefferson

Bible was published after Jefferson's death in 1895 under the title *The Life and Morals of Jesus of Nazareth Extracted Textually from the Gospels.*

Jesus was not just a moral teacher; He was so much more. Not only did Jesus teach ethical values of love, forgiveness, respect, and character; He also raised the dead, healed the sick, and set people free from their afflictions. When Thomas Jefferson removed the miracles from his version of the Bible, he inadvertently removed the element of faith required to be a follower of God. Becoming a Christian requires that we believe God is the source of all our redemption, renewal, and restoration. We must trust Him with all things, and we must trust that He can do all things. God calls us to faith—to believe in the impossible—and it's an awesome calling!

> *God calls us to faith—to believe in the impossible—and it's an awesome calling!*

1. *Do you think it's possible to believe in God without believing in the miraculous? Why or why not?*

2. *How would the Bible be different without any miracles? How would the life of Jesus be different without any miracles?*

One powerful healing miracle that was left out of Jefferson's Bible is found in Matthew 17. Jesus had just taken Peter, James, and John up a high mountain. While they were gathered together, Jesus was transfigured before them. His face shone bright as the sun and His clothes became radiant. In this miraculous scene, Moses and Elijah talked with Jesus. Following this unforgettable encounter, the very first thing Jesus did was to heal a young boy by setting him free from an afflicting spirit.

3. *Read Matthew 17:14–21. How did the concerned father approach Jesus? What did he ask of Jesus?*

4. *How did Jesus react when He learned that the disciples could not heal the boy (v. 17)?*

5. Why couldn't the disciples heal the boy (v. 20)?

Many who heard Jesus' teaching were amazed. They noted He taught as someone with power, not like the Pharisees of the time. The Gospels highlight some of the individuals who had profound encounters with Jesus. One of them was a Roman centurion.

*6. Read **Matthew 8:5–13**. What did the centurion ask of Jesus (vv. 5—6)? What was Jesus' response (v. 7)? Does anything surprise you about the centurion's statement or Jesus' answer?*

7. How did the centurion respond to Jesus' offer to come to his home (v. 8)? Why was this response so surprising and pleasing to Jesus?

8. *What inspires you most about the story of the Roman centurion? What, specifically, can you do to grow in your faith?*

Jesus was not just a teacher, but the Son of God. Following Him requires us to continually grow in faith and trust Him for the miraculous.

Digging Deeper

Psalm 37 encourages people to maintain patience during troubling times. Read Psalm 37:3–8. Rewrite this passage below. Circle all the verbs that direct us in our relationship with God. On a scale of 1 to 10 (10 being the most difficult), how hard is it for you to follow all the directive advice in this passage?

Bonus Activity

Share your faith online. Log on to a Web site and share your faith through a message board or blog (an online Web diary). You can join a discussion online at many ministry sites, as well as through some of your favorite Christian magazine or writers' sites. You may even want to start your own blog to share what God is doing in your life.

Eight

Tapping into His Power

Light tomorrow with today.

ELIZABETH BARRETT BROWNING

More than three thousand people joined the crowd the night the first lightbulb was displayed. They came from all over the United States just hoping to get a glimpse of Thomas and his lightbulb. Traveling to the exhibition in the train that chugged over the New Jersey hills, people sat patiently, imagining what it would be like—a world lit by electric lightbulbs. Up until this time, streets and homes had been lit by gas lamps that radiated a poisonous gas, became really hot, and weren't always reliable. People gathered together, filled with curiosity.

Born in Ohio in 1847, Thomas Edison was the youngest of seven children. With little formal education, his mother taught Thomas the basics of math, science, and English. Always curious by nature, he continued to learn on his own. Like many young teens, Edison began working at an early age, selling newspapers and treats to travelers at a nearby railroad. By the age of sixteen, Edison became a telegrapher and traveled the country with his newfound profession. But his curiosity for learning and making things better led him to begin inventing.

Thomas Edison received a patent for an electric vote recorder—an invention that turned out to be a commercial failure—but he kept on inventing. He developed the phonograph, a device that played recorded sound. Edison went on to develop the first central power station and the kinetoscope (which played motion pictures). He employed his skill in fashioning an improved battery for electric cars and made many other improvements to existing inventions. However, the invention that made Thomas Edison famous was the incandescent electric light. (It turns out Edison was not the first to invent an electric lightbulb; he just found better and longer-lasting materials for the bulb.)

God is the one who gives us strength, hope, and life. Apart from Him, we can do nothing.

It was Thomas Edison's introduction of his improved lightbulb that drew several thousand people together on New Year's Eve in 1879. Did people come for the inventor or the invention? Probably both. With Edison's creative inventiveness, the world shifted into the age of electricity, and Edison was at the forefront of developing the electric industry. Today, we still feel the effects of Edison's ingenuity. Just think about the last time you tried to turn something on only to discover it wasn't plugged in. No power source means no power. But it's not just everyday items like hairdryers, curling irons, and microwaves that need a power source. We need one, too! As believers, God is our power source. He is the one who gives us strength, hope, and life. Apart from Him, we can do nothing.

1. *In the space below, make a list of five inventions run by electricity that would be the hardest for you to live without.*

2. *What role do you think natural curiosity and imagination played in Edison's ability to invent? Do you enjoy creating, inventing, or finding solutions to problems? Why or why not?*

From beginning to end, the Bible is filled with stories about the power of God. God spoke creation into existence with mere words. God is the one who preserved the life of Noah and his family on a wooden boat. It was the power of God that allowed Sarah, the wife of Abraham, to become pregnant in old age. When Pharaoh refused to allow God's people, the Israelites, to be set free, God displayed His power in a series of miraculous plagues. Throughout the Old and New Testaments, it's hard to read very many pages without seeing the power of God on display. He can do anything!

3. Read **Jeremiah 32:17** and write the verse in the space below. Why is it important to remember this truth about God before we begin to pray?

Psalm 18 is a beautiful testimony to the power and faithfulness of God. The psalm (a song of praise written by David) thanks God for His strength and power, in which we can take refuge and find protection and safety. David thanked God for rescuing him in his time of trouble and responding to his cry for help. The psalm is a reminder that God will move heaven and earth in order to rescue one of His children.

4. Read **Psalm 18**. What comfort do you find within this chapter for your own faith journey?

5. Read the following Scriptures that describe God's power. Match the reference with the appropriate Scripture.

Scripture Reference	Scripture
1 Chronicles 29:12	"Wealth and honor come from you; you are the ruler of all things. In your hands are strength and power to exalt and give strength to all."
2 Chronicles 25:8	"One thing God has spoken, two things have I heard: that you, O God, are strong."
Job 42:2	"[You] formed the mountains by your power, having armed yourself with strength."
Psalm 62:11	"I know that you can do all things; no plan of yours can be thwarted."
Psalm 65:6	"Even if you go and fight courageously in battle, God will overthrow you before the enemy, for God has the power to help or to overthrow."

6. Which of these verses is the most meaningful to you? Why?

7. What kinds of situations tend to "unplug" you from the truth of who God is and the power He has over all things?

8. What steps can you take—including prayer, studying the Bible, and serving others—to remain "plugged in" to God and His power?

Apart from God, we can do nothing. God is the one who is the source of everything. To become all God wants us to be, we need to remain "plugged in" to Him.

Digging Deeper

Staying plugged in to God is a constant necessity for Christians. Read John 15:1–8. Who did Jesus say He is? What part does God play in this analogy? How do you see this analogy as true in your own life? How fruitful are you? In what ways do you struggle to remain in Christ?

Bonus Activity

We need to stay plugged in to God's power. However, in our modern world, we need to unplug from electric power whenever possible in order to care for the environment. Over the course of the next week, pay attention to your lifestyle and home. Are there any areas where you can cut back your electricity usage? Can you turn your refrigerator to a more energy-saving level or set the water temperature of your clothes washer to warm or cold instead of hot? Are you making sure your dishwasher is truly full before you run it? Can you turn down the temperature of your water heater? Have you switched to compact, fluorescent bulbs? Small changes like these can make a big difference in your electric bill and the environment!

9/1/92

Nine

Stories of Great Faith

*If you wish to possess finally all that is
yours, give yourself entirely to God.*

HADEWIJCH OF BRABANT

*Have you had
an encounter w/ God?*

Have you ever sat and listened to the stories of people who have
had a profound encounter with God? It's amazing to see the great
lengths to which God will go in order to reveal Himself to us. John
Wesley, the founder of Methodism, related one of the most significant encounters of his life; it happened on May 24, 1738:

> In the evening I went very unwillingly to a society in Aldersgate
> Street, where one was reading Luther's preface to the Epistle to the
> Romans. About a quarter before nine, while he was describing the
> change which God works in the heart through faith in Christ, I felt
> my heart strangely warmed. I felt I did trust in Christ, Christ alone,
> for salvation; and an assurance was given me that He had taken away
> my sins, even mine, and saved me from the law of sin and death.
>
> I began to pray with all my might for those who had in a more
> especial manner despitefully used me and persecuted me. I then
> testified openly to all there what I now first felt in my heart. But

it was not long before the enemy suggested, "This cannot be faith; for where is thy joy?" Then was I taught that peace and victory over sin are essential to faith in the Captain of our salvation; but that, as to the transports of joy that usually attend the beginning of it, especially in those who have mourned deeply, God sometimes giveth, sometimes withholdeth them, according to the counsels of His own will.

Wesley went on to describe the next day, "The moment I awaked, 'Jesus, Master,' was in my heart and in my mouth; and I found all my strength lay in keeping my eye fixed upon Him, and my soul waiting on Him continually."[2]

Wesley later became known as a circuit-riding preacher. He shared the good news of what God had done in his life and challenged others to follow Jesus. It's estimated that he traveled more than 100,000 miles around England and preached an estimated 40,000 sermons. Yet, Wesley was focused on not just teaching the good news of Jesus, but also demonstrating it by caring for the whole person. He founded homes for orphans, schools for the poor, opposed slavery, and published countless resources to help people understand Scripture.

> *No matter what your age or stage in life, God has great plans for you—plans beyond your wildest imaginings.*

Today, as a result of his methodical approach to teaching Scripture, millions of Methodists around the globe worship God.

Stories like John Wesley's are encouraging. It's awesome to think about what God can do through someone's life! Have you spent time thinking about all God wants to do through your life? No matter what your age or stage in life, God has great plans for you—plans beyond your wildest imaginings. You may be tempted to think what you're doing right now doesn't have significance, but when you place your life before God, anything is possible.

1. *How did you first come to know God? What was your experience?*

2. *Do you tend to openly share with others the story of how you met God or do you tend to be more reserved in sharing your story? Why?*

3. *How has your life been changed by knowing God?*

Imagine

One powerful story of a life being transformed is found in Acts 8. Philip was spreading the good news of Jesus when the Holy Spirit worked through him in an unexpected way to change the life of a foreigner.

4. Read *Acts 8:26–40*. What did the angel instruct Philip to do (vv. 26–28)? go South

5. Have you ever felt compelled by the Holy Spirit to do something unusual? What was the result?

Prayed for Gene

6. What did Philip do and say in order to share the good news of Jesus with the eunuch (vv. 30–38)?
Heard the eunuch reading in Isaiah - asking Do yu understand Philip told him about Jesus and baptized him

Prophesy of Jesus -
Fulfilled in Matt 26:62
mark 15:3-5 Luke 23:9
John 19: 8-10

7. *What principles of how to share the good news are demonstrated in this passage?*

obedience and responding to God's
leading

building relationships

* knowing the scripture and
* able to teach or share
the gospel

8. *Why do you think it's important to share the good news of what God has done in your life? Have you ever seen anyone's life impacted by what you've shared? If so, describe.*

We are to be witnesses
and lead people to the
Lord.

> *Whether you realize it or not, you have a great story of faith. While it may not be as dramatic as some, your story is unique and God wants you to use it to share the good news of who He is and all that He has done.*

Digging Deeper

King David wrote Psalm 19 with the intention of celebrating the Word of God. Read **Psalm 19:7.** Why do you think it's important to meditate on God's Word? How has studying Scripture changed your perspective of others? Specific situations? Life? Share a time when Scripture has "revived your soul."

Bonus Activity

Organize a movie marathon. Invite members of the group to spend an afternoon watching films and discussing spiritually related topics. Consider watching *Wall-E* and discussing what it means to avoid overconsumption and care for the earth. Check out *Iron Man* and discuss what redemption in someone's life really looks like. Or select your own film and conversation starter. Add some snacks, popcorn, and comfy chairs, and have a blast together!

Conquering the Impossible

God can do more than you ever

dreamed, but to embrace all God

wants you to do, you must choose

to walk in faith and faithfulness.

Ten

Nothing Is Impossible for God

I do not at all understand the mystery of grace—only that it meets us where we are but does not leave us where it found us.

ANNE LAMOTT

There is a story about a man who was hiking up a cliff when he slipped and fell off. On the way down, he grabbed onto a tree branch and held on as tightly as he could.

"Is anyone up there?" the man cried out, hopeful that someone would hear him.

"I am here. I am the Lord. Do you believe Me?" a voice echoed.

"Yes, Lord, I believe. I really believe, but I can't hang on much longer," the man said, his arms weakening.

"That's all right. If you really believe, you have nothing to worry about. I will save you. Just let go of the branch," the voice responded.

A moment of pause, then: "Is anyone else up there?"[1]

This lighthearted tale illustrates the challenge all of us face when it comes to issues of faith. Usually, it's fairly easy to say we believe or that we have faith; but when we find ourselves hanging on to a branch on the side of the cliff of life, it can be a whole lot more difficult to *really* believe. The very nature of faith invites us to embrace with our hearts and minds that which seems out of reach. Faith is not about what's possible; faith operates in the realm of the impossible. Faith begins when our abilities end. Faith comes to life when all our other options have failed. Faith invites us to believe in what we can't see and hope in what we have yet to experience.

> *The very nature of faith invites us to embrace with our hearts and minds that which seems out of reach.*

As Augustine once said, "God does not expect us to submit our faith to Him without reason, but the very limits of our reason make faith a necessity."

1. *Have you ever been in a situation like that of the man on the side of the cliff? If so, was it easy to trust God in that moment or, like the man, did you wonder, "Is there anyone else out there?"*

2. *Why do you think so many people ask, "Is there anyone else out there?" when they find themselves in a sticky situation?*

3. *Would you say faith comes easily for you? Why or why not?*

Throughout His ministry, Jesus worked countless miracles. He opened blind eyes and deaf ears. He healed the paralyzed and those with leprosy. Yet, despite the many miraculous acts, the Bible says there was one location where He didn't do many miracles.

4. *Read **Matthew 13:53–58**. In this passage, what was Jesus' location (v. 54)? How did the people of this area respond to Jesus?*

5. Why didn't Jesus perform many miracles in this particular area (v. 58)? Do you think Jesus would have performed more miracles in this area if the people had believed? Why or why not?

Not only does faith play an essential role in all God wants to do in our lives, faith is also essential to pleasing God.

6. Read **Hebrews 11:6** and write the passage in the space below. Why do you think faith is so pleasing to God?

Faith is not only essential in pleasing God, but faith is also essential in prayer.

7. Read *James 1:1–7*. Why is it important to "not doubt" but rather ask in faith (vv. 6—7)? Have you ever prayed without faith? What was the result?

8. What attitudes or actions do you need to change to allow faith to be effective in your life?

Faith invites us to step beyond ourselves and truly believe in God with our whole selves. Through faith, we have the opportunity to watch the God of the universe do the impossible in our lives, as well as in the lives of those we love.

Digging Deeper

Read 2 Kings 4:1–7. What did Elisha ask of the woman? What was the result of her faithfulness? Have you ever seen something miraculous come from being faithful?

Bonus Activity

Whom do you pray for on a regular basis? Family members? Friends? Neighbors? Government leaders? Have you ever thought about creating a prayer scrapbook? Simply glue photos and images of the people for whom you pray into a small journal. Make your design as simple or as elaborate as you like. Then, pray through your journal each day.

Eleven

Believing in the Impossible

When I look at the galaxies on a clear night—when
I look at the incredible brilliance of creation, and
think that this is what God is like, then instead
of feeling intimidated and diminished by it, I am
enlarged . . . I rejoice that I am a part of it.

MADELEINE L'ENGLE

Heavy storm clouds hung on the horizon all afternoon. As the sun dipped below the horizon, the clouds crept across the sky. The wind steadily increased. A few water droplets from a wave splashed on the deck of the boat. The storm had begun.

The men knew what to do. Some of them had grown up on these waters. Fishing wasn't just their passion, it was also their profession; or had been, up until the time they encountered the Rabbi. He had turned their worlds upside down—everything they knew and believed had changed.

As night began to cast its darkest shadows, one of the men saw something on the water. It wasn't another boat. It wasn't anything they had seen before. It was a man walking on the water! Soon, all eyes were on what they could only guess was a ghost.

"Take courage! It is I. Don't be afraid," the familiar voice announced (Matthew 14:27).

Was it really the Rabbi?

Peter was the first to speak up. "Lord, if it's you, tell me to come to you on the water" (14:28).

The ghost, the Rabbi, the whatever-it-was answered with a single word, "Come" (14:29).

Though he felt weak in the knees, Peter's heart told his body to do what his mind screamed was impossible. He stared intently into the loving face of his Rabbi as he stepped from the boat. The firm sensation of the water beneath his feet seemed natural. One step. Two steps. Three steps. The wind gusted across Peter's face. Turning his head, he lost sight of the Rabbi as the sea quickly began to swallow his body.

In their hearts, they knew beyond a shadow of doubt that Jesus was the Son of God.

"Lord, save me!" Peter screamed (14:30).

Within a split second, Jesus grabbed Peter's hand.

"You of little faith. Why did you doubt?" Jesus said, gently but firmly (14:31).

Peter was speechless. Wouldn't you be, too?

The scriptural account of this story illustrates a profound moment of faith in the lives of Peter and the disciples. The response of the disciples was to worship Jesus. In their hearts, they knew beyond a shadow of doubt that Jesus was the Son of God.

1. Read *Matthew 14:22–33*. How did Peter respond to Jesus (v. 28)?
   What do you think your response would have been?

   Bid me come

   I wouldn't have left the boat.

2. What role did faith play in this story?

   huge role —

3. What adjectives would you use to describe the tone of Jesus' voice
   when He said, "You of little faith, why did you doubt?" (v. 31).

   *I think he was loving, because
   Peter had tried — he was encouraging
   him — why did you doubt.*

In the Gospel of John, we read the story of Jesus' interaction with a Samaritan woman at a well. The scene is unexpected because Jews and Samaritans did not associate with each other.

4. Read **John 4:1–30**. *What did Jesus ask of the Samaritan woman (v. 7)? Do you think the woman was surprised by Jesus' request (v. 9)? Why or why not?*

Asked for water

Yes - Jews didn't speak to Samaritans

Samaritans believed there place of Worship Was Mt Gerazim not Jerusalem

5. *How did Jesus respond to the woman (v. 10)?*

He would give her "living" water

Jesus sat at a well and asked a woman for a drink, but only a few moments later the woman became spiritually thirsty. She asked Jesus for access to the "living water" He described. At this point, Jesus addressed a big issue in this woman's life.

6. *What did Jesus ask of the woman (v. 16)? How did the woman respond (v. 17)? What was the real story the woman was trying to avoid telling Jesus (v. 18)?*

Jesus had exposed what was really going on in the woman's life. She may have been tempted to leave or even deny the truth. Instead, she chose to recognize that Jesus was a prophet.

7. *What did Jesus reveal to the woman about His identity (v. 26)? What was the woman's response (vv. 28–29)?*

That He was the Messiah

8. *In what ways are you being challenged to take greater risks in faith and obedience?*

> Job 9:8
> He alone has spread out the heavens and marches on the waves of the sea.

W   *to*
in   *n*
ris   *r.*

Digging Deeper

The Old Testament contains numerous references to God's control of nature. On several occasions, the Bible presents an image of God walking on water. Read **Job 9:8** and **Psalm 77:19**. What did Jesus' walking on water suggest about His identity? What does this reveal about the power of God? What does this reveal about God's ability to do the impossible?

Bonus Activity

Support a local artist. Do you have a budding musician or artist in your faith community? Find out when their next concert or showcase will be and put it on your calendar. Invite a few friends. Choose to actively support this talented artist by attending, purchasing a product, and through prayer. Your support can mean more than you know!

Twelve

Called to the Impossible

*What are Christians put into the world for except
to do the impossible in the strength of God?*

GENERAL S. C. ARMSTRONG

Chuck Colson served as President Richard Nixon's special counsel
from 1969 to 1973. After the Watergate scandal made headline news,
Colson resigned from the White House. Though he was never pros-
ecuted for any charges regarding the Watergate cover-up, he did
plead guilty to obstruction of justice in another case that earned him
more than six months in prison.

While facing arrest during the Watergate scandal, a friend gave
Chuck Colson a copy of C. S. Lewis's *Mere Christianity*. As a result,
Colson became a Christian. Upon his release, Colson felt compelled
to share the good news of Jesus with those still in prison. He founded
Prison Fellowship, which has become the largest prison outreach
organization in the world. Its branches include Project Angel Tree,
Operation Starting Line, InnerChange Freedom Initiative, and Jus-
tice Fellowship.

At one point, Colson was offered the opportunity to speak to an assembly at San Quentin Prison. He was thrilled at the chance to serve and reach the lost. Out of a prison population of twenty-two hundred, more than three hundred opted to listen to Colson's sermon. Just days before he was scheduled to speak, a cache of weapons was found inside the prison; the prison went into lockdown status. Instead of three hundred participants, only a handful of prisoners were allowed to attend the meeting.

On the day of the assembly, just before he got up to speak, Colson spotted a video camera in the back corner of the room. He wondered if the session was being recorded for the prison library. He passionately shared his testimony to the handful of men and the camera—praying for the impossible. Following his heartfelt, fervent talk, Colson told the prison chaplain he was disappointed so few men had been allowed to attend. The chaplain explained that the unexpected lockdown had caused the administration to decide to record the sermon. The video would be broadcast twice the next day to every single cell—once in the morning and once at night.

We serve a God for whom nothing is beyond His redemption or restoration.

Colson's sermon not only aired twice, but twelve times over the upcoming weeks. Due to the lockdown, all twenty-two hundred inmates were able to hear and watch Colson share the good news of Jesus.

Chuck Colson's story is a powerful reminder that nothing is impossible with God. We may look at our own lives and think that something we've done has disqualified us from making a difference in God's kingdom. But we serve a God for whom nothing is beyond His redemption or restoration. When we choose to follow God and obey His commands, it's amazing to think of all He can do in us and through us.

1. What surprises you most about Chuck Colson's story?

It seemed that he wouldn't have a successful meeting because only a few could attend.
It was good he saw the camera and preached fervently.

Apart from prayer, we can never imagine all that God wants to do in our lives. It's through our relationship with God—talking to Him about our hopes, dreams, and desires, as well as His hopes, dreams, and desires for us—that we discover where God is leading us.

2. In the space below, make a list of five adjectives that describe your current prayer life.

spontaneous -

3. In the space below, make a list of five adjectives that you would like to be true of your own prayer life.

More faith

Imagine

Many Bible scholars believe the prayers offered by Jewish religious leaders during the time Jesus lived were very formal. It is believed they often repeated a set of sayings or portions of Scripture such as the Psalms. In addition, prayers were spoken in formal Hebrew. Yet, the everyday language of the Jews was Aramaic.

Jesus' prayers must have stood out! Why? Because when Jesus prayed He did so in Aramaic, and He prayed casually and conversationally. He offered His personal concerns to God.

4. Read *Matthew 6:5–15*. What are some characteristics of the way Jesus instructed His followers to pray? (For example: prayer that is heartfelt, sincere, and personal.)

Pray privately – not for show
Pray sincerely –
Don't be pious or try to use eloquent words – pray simple

Luke 11 begins with Jesus praying. When He finished, one of the disciples asked Jesus to teach on prayer. Jesus recited a shorter version of the Lord's Prayer found in Matthew 6. Then, Jesus offered a compelling story about the power of prayer.

5. Read *Luke 11:1–13*. In the story about the neighbor in need, why do you think the sleeping man got up and provided the bread (v. 8)? What does this story suggest about how we pray (v. 9)?

Because the person kept knocking.

Keep praying and asking –
Abraham ask the Lord about how many people in Sodom & Gor. He quit asking at ten. The Lord didn't leave until Abram quit asking – ?? Genesis 18:16-33

While the story of the sleeping neighbor is often used to illustrate the importance of being courageous in prayer, it also points to something else. In ancient Israel, the issue of honor was not based on the individual as much as it was the community. When a visitor came to town, his treatment was reflective not of just his host, but of the entire village. In the story Jesus told, the need for bread is not just the host's concern, but the village's concern. This is the reason the host knows he can go to his friend at midnight and receive his request. The sudden need for bread is not about a meal; it's about the deeper issue of honor.

Luke 11:8 says, "I tell you, though he will not get up and give him the bread because he is his friend, yet because of the man's *boldness* he will get up and give him as much as he needs" (emphasis added). The word translated *boldness* in this verse is the Greek word *anaideia*, which can also be translated as *shameless*. In other words, the host went to this particular friend because he knew the man was "shameless." He was a man of good character. Why is this significant? Because, just as the host knew his neighbor would respond because of his good character, so we, too, can go confidently to God, knowing that His response will be based not on our pleas or performance, but on His goodness.

6. *How does this interpretation of the passage change the way you understand Jesus' teaching?*

In the verses following this passage, Jesus continued teaching about prayer. He explained that we are to ask, seek, and knock; and our God, who is good, will answer our requests.

7. Reread *Luke 11:9–13*. How does the knowledge that answers to prayer are based not on the way you pray, but on the character of God, affect the way you think about prayer?

Abraham
Gen 18:26-33

8. Reflecting on this study, what do you believe God is calling you to imagine? What do you think God wants to do in your life that is more than you ever dreamed?

I think imagination is faith.
Heb 11:6 Without faith it is impossible to please God!
Matt 9:29 According to your faith be it unto you.

As you seek God and grow in your relationship with Him, you will find yourself growing in faith. You'll discover God wants to do more than you ever imagined; not because of anything you do, but simply because of who He is.

Digging Deeper

Like most people, Paul understood what it felt like to be anxious. He left great advice for the anxious in his letter to the church of Philippi. Read **Philippians 4:6**. To what or whom do you turn when you are anxious? According to this verse, to whom should we turn? Have you seen this to be fruitful in your own life? Why or why not?

Bonus Activity

Psalm 91 is the only psalm attributed to Moses. Look up **Psalm 91:15–16**. Rewrite these two verses on note cards and dedicate the next week to memorizing them. Prayerfully go to God with any heartaches, troubles, joys, or thanksgiving.

Leader's Guide

Chapter 1: Embrace Your Imagination

Focus: *The things God has in store for us are beyond our wildest imaginations.*

1. *Encourage participants to have fun with this quiz. Remind them that it's an enjoyable way to help them think about how much they're using their imaginations at this age and stage of life.*

2. *Children can come up with the most creative games. Encourage participants to share what they remember from their childhood games and role-playing. If they liked to play classroom, did they prefer being the teacher or the student? If they liked to pretend they were in a kitchen, did they like to cook or serve or eat? Have fun with this question.*

3. *Although not always immediately apparent, there are many times in daily life when we have the opportunity to use our imaginations. Designing products and projects for work, home, and church involves imagination. Developing creative solutions to everyday problems often requires creativity and imagination. Often, playing with children also employs the imagination.*

4. *Jesus assured His followers that He was going to prepare a place for them and they would be together again.*

5. *Answers will vary, but Jesus was describing heaven to His disciples. It is possible they tried to imagine how grand and beautiful the place prepared for them would be.*

6. Answers will vary. Encourage the participants to share little blurbs about what they imagine heaven to be. Describe the beauty, the people, the sights and sounds.

7. After hearing Jesus tell them about betrayal and denials, they were probably a little shaken up. The assurance of Jesus' return and a brief description of their future home would have been comforting.

8. Answers will vary, but God is preparing a place for us all. Jesus is the way to get to the Father and experience the place Jesus is preparing for us.

Digging Deeper

Heaven won't be like an earthly temple, because God and Jesus are the temple. There will be no need for light because God's glory illuminates everything. Heaven will be beautiful and awe-inspiring. God loves us so much that He has prepared such a place for us to be with Him forever.

Chapter 2: The Beauty of Story

Focus: *Stories are powerful tools for teaching spiritual lessons and illustrating truths. They invoke our imaginations and cause us to think differently.*

1. Encourage participants to share their favorite children's stories and books. You may even want to keep a running list of some of the different titles for the bonus activity at the end of this lesson.

2. *Great storytelling, compelling characters, colorful dialogue, surprising twists in plot, and rich life-lessons are the common characteristics of great stories.*

3. *Answers will vary, but it's interesting to note the characteristics of a great story are often the same, regardless of audience or age.*

4. *One of the primary lessons from this story is, despite our best intentions, our involvement can actually make things worse if we don't know the whole situation or fully understand the person we're trying to help. The story also reminds us to discover the best way to help others before diving in.*

5. *Answers will vary, but most participants can think of a time when good-intentioned involvement didn't result in the best of outcomes. Participants may also be able to think of times when someone tried to help them but things didn't turn out as expected.*

6. *One son said he would not work in the vineyard, but he did. The other said he would, but didn't. The contrast is between the two sons' words and actions. One repented and changed; the other did not.*

7. *The first son represented the tax collectors and prostitutes who disobeyed the law, but repented. The second son represented the religious leaders who said they were obeying the law, but really didn't obey God's message.*

8. *The listeners were probably shocked to hear Jesus applauding tax collectors and prostitutes for their repentance. The religious leaders probably expected to be the first to enter God's kingdom. Answers will vary as to whether participants identify more with the first or second son.*

Digging Deeper

The "treasure" and the "pearl" spoken of in this passage represent the kingdom of heaven. The men sold everything they had to keep the valuables. They made a great sacrifice because they knew what they had found was a real treasure. Answers will vary.

Chapter 3: The Wonder of God

Focus: *God is almighty, powerful, and truly awesome. Reflecting on the wonder of who God is and all He has done strengthens our faith.*

1. *This icebreaker question is designed to get participants sharing and laughing.*

2. *Answers will vary, but don't forget about phrases such as "absolutely," "24-7," and "with all due respect."*

3. *Answers will vary. Consider **amazing**, **perfect**, or **love**. Sometimes people overuse the words amazing and perfect to the point that **everything** is amazing or perfect. And sometimes people will overuse the word love to the extent that they "love" every little thing they encounter.*

4. *Answers will vary. God is all-powerful, omnipotent, and almighty. Lightning, thunder, rain, snow, ice, clouds, and the sun are just a few of the elements in nature that display the wonder and awe of God's power and creativity.*

5. *Answers will vary, but it's truly amazing to consider the power and creativity of God.*

6. *Answers will vary.*

7. *Answers will vary. It is easy for us to take God's wonder and majesty for granted. We get so caught up in daily life, we forget to take time to appreciate and stand in awe of the power and beauty of God.*

8. *Answers will vary, but God's power can be encouraging and comforting as we take on daily life. Knowing we have a God who controls all of nature and is also on our side is reassuring.*

Digging Deeper

God's thoughts are all-powerful and all-knowing, whereas our thoughts all too often concern ourselves and those around us. Our thoughts pale in comparison with God's. Answers will vary, but it is comforting to know that God is in control; He is not limited by human faculties.

Bonus Activity

The answers to the two riddles are: (1) The horse's name is Friday; and (2) the wind won't blow the smoke in any direction because electric trains don't create smoke.

Chapter 4:
Putting Yourself in Someone Else's Shoes

> **Focus:** *We can use our imaginations to put ourselves in other people's shoes and develop compassion for them.*

1. *Answers will vary. The young man could have felt rejected, unwanted, or debased. He could have felt unworthy to be in their church. Without the warm, loving embrace of someone at the church, he could have gotten a tainted view of God, church, or Christians.*

2. *Answers will vary.*

3. *Sometimes the people who walk into our lives, communities, or even our churches are so different from us we have difficulty connecting to them. We may meet someone who is socially awkward, scantily clad, or has a shady past and reputation.*

4. *Answers may vary, but by loving others just as they are, we have the opportunity to show God's love.*

5. *Answers will vary, but the women probably never imagined such loss and pain.*

6. *Boaz probably imagined Ruth lived a poor, impoverished life, since she was forced to glean the fields.*

7. *Boaz invited her to glean from his fields. He offered her water and gave her food. Boaz instructed his harvesters to leave food in the field for Ruth to gather. This is significant because, though Ruth*

95

was of a lower class. Boaz respected her and what she had done for Naomi.

8. *Answers will vary. Only by seeing situations through the eyes of others or experiencing them ourselves can we begin to feel and understand the hardships faced by others.*

Digging Deeper

Boaz bought the property Naomi was selling and married Ruth. He went out of his way to accept and show compassion for the women. Their reactions were probably shock and thanksgiving.

Chapter 5: Aware of the Needs

Focus: *God calls us to meet the needs of others. Sometimes serving others and making a difference will involve finding creative solutions and using our imaginations to help solve problems.*

1. *Answers will vary. Someone experiencing scenario A could respond by sharing her meal or offering to purchase the friend's meal. Someone in scenario B could respond by purchasing clothes, meals, or school supplies for the children, or offering free babysitting. Someone in scenario C could offer to take some of the pastor's daily jobs off his hands, or purchase a vacation or get-away for him. In all scenarios, prayer is welcome and needed.*

2. *Answers will vary, but scenarios like these come up frequently. The differences are in how or if we respond.*

3. *Answers will vary, but everyone has been through times when they were emotionally, financially, or physically drained. The people who step into our lives and offer to help can have a big impact.*

4. *The angel told Paul that no lives would be lost on the boat. Paul still needed to stand trial before Caesar.*

5. *They showed "unusual kindness" (Acts 28:2) and built them a fire and welcomed them. They honored the visitors in many ways. The chief official of the island welcomed them into his home. When the shipwreck victims were about to leave, they were given the supplies they needed.*

6. *Jesus used a parable to illustrate the difference between sheep and goats. Sheep are those who feed the hungry, offer drink to the thirsty, clothe those who cannot afford clothes, watch over the sick, and visit the prisoner. The goats are those who see the same needs but refuse to offer assistance.*

7. *Being a sheep is more challenging because it means getting involved emotionally, physically, and financially. A goat can see a need and simply pass by, but a sheep uses personal resources, including time, money, and energy, to help those in need. We can feel tempted to behave like goats and ignore the needs of others when business, self-centeredness, and selfishness get the best of us.*

8. *Answers will vary. Encourage participants to think specifically and practically. Is there someone in your community with a need? Is there a single mom in the church who is going through a difficult time? Does someone have a neighbor who lost a job? Consider developing a plan, as a group, to be the feet and hands of Jesus to someone in need.*

Digging Deeper

Paul and Silas released a slave girl from the power of an evil spirit. The owners of the girl were angry and brought Paul and Silas before the authorities, who imprisoned them. While they were in prison, an earthquake struck. Rather than escaping when the earthquake opened a way, Paul and Silas prayed and sang hymns to God while the others listened. They showed compassion for the jailer by not trying to escape when they had the chance. Paul also stopped the jailer from hurting himself, shared the good news with him, and baptized him. Upon the apostles' release from prison, the jailer took them to his own home, washed the men's wounds, and set a meal before them.

Chapter 6: Unexpectedly Used by God

Focus: *No matter how unqualified or undeserving we may feel, God wants to use us. As He did with Moses, He may use us to set people free.*

1. *Answers will vary, but many people may be shocked that he tried to smuggle the Bibles; even more so that he got away with it.*

2. *Answers will vary, but many may have experienced financial problems or physical ailments that only God could cure.*

3. *Answers will vary, but usually the toughest situations allow for the biggest growth in faith. The harder the situation, the more we grow and learn from it. Faith-testing times can be intimidating and frustrating, but very rewarding.*

4. *God asked Moses to go to Pharaoh and bring His people out of Egypt. Answers will vary, but many people may be fearful or feel unworthy or too unimportant to do what God asks of them. Moses asked, "Who am I, that I should go to Pharaoh and bring the Israelites out of Egypt?" (Exodus 3:11). Moses second concern was, "Suppose I go to the Israelites and say to them, 'The God of your fathers has sent me to you,' and they ask me, 'What is his name?' Then what shall I tell them?" (3:13). God promised Moses that He would be with him. He assured Moses that the Israelites would worship God on the mountain after they had been delivered. God also told Moses to tell the Israelites, "I AM has sent me to you" (3:14). Through this encounter, God revealed Himself to Moses and all humankind as "I AM."*

5. *Moses said he was not a good speaker and shouldn't be the one to convince Pharaoh to release the Israelites. God reminded Moses that He created human mouths and the ability to speak. God told Moses to go and promised to teach him what to say.*

6. *Answers*

Scripture Reference	Plague That Occurred
Exodus 7:19	Plague of blood
Exodus 8:6	Plague of frogs
Exodus 8:16	Plague of gnats
Exodus 8:21	Plague of flies
Exodus 9:3	Plague on livestock
Exodus 9:8–9	Plague of boils
Exodus 9:18	Plague of hail
Exodus 10:4–5	Plague of locusts
Exodus 10:21–23	Plague of darkness
Exodus 11:4–5	Plague on the firstborn

Answers will vary as to which plaques are scariest, grossest, or most disturbing.

7. *While Pharaoh was affected by all of the other plagues, only the last hit close to home—it took the life of his firstborn child. The loss and pain must have been significant for Pharaoh, just as it was for all the parents who lost children that night. While Scripture does not clearly say what changed in Pharaoh's heart, something obviously did. Pharaoh recognized that his obedience to God's command to let the people go was his only option.*

8. *This is significant because Pharaoh was probably brokenhearted at the loss of his son. For a brief moment, he may have seen a glimpse of hope in the God of Moses and Aaron. One can only speculate as to Moses' and Aaron's responses to the Pharaoh's request for blessing. He may have seemed a broken man. Whatever their response, this was the first time Moses and Aaron had seen Pharaoh in this condition.*

Digging Deeper

Answers will vary, but often God's power and grace are most obvious in our lives when we're at our weakest. Delighting in a struggle is difficult.

Chapter 7: Growing in Faith

Focus: *Jesus was not just a teacher, but the Son of God. Following Him requires us to continually grow in faith and trust Him for the miraculous.*

1. *It's not possible to believe in God without believing in the miraculous. God is not limited by human standards. He exists outside human boundaries. God is all-powerful. God has infinite wisdom. God is omnipresent.*

2. *The Bible is full of miracles—from the story of Noah and the ark, to the provision of manna in the desert, to the virgin birth of Jesus. The Bible would be radically different without any miracles. It would not represent God for who He truly is. It would be a lot thinner. And the life of Christ would be reduced to mere teachings, lacking in power and failing to fulfill Old Testament prophecy.*

3. *The man knelt before Jesus. This signified humility and a pleading desire to have Jesus help his suffering son. He asked Jesus to have mercy on his son. He explained that the boy had seizures and often threw himself into the fire and water. The man had taken the boy to the disciples, but they were unable to help him.*

4. *Jesus expressed frustration. He called the generation "unbelieving" and "perverse." He asked how long He'd be with them and how long He'd have to put up with them. He proceeded to deliver the boy Himself.*

5. *The smallness of the disciples' faith affected their ability to help the boy. Just as a mustard seed grows into a massive tree, even small*

portions of faith can become a world-changing power. (In regard to the exorcized demon, some translations add verse 21: "But this kind does not go out except by prayer and fasting.")

6. *The centurion did not actually ask Jesus a question. Instead, he merely told Jesus his servant was at home, paralyzed and in terrible suffering. Jesus announced He would go and heal the servant. The exchange is incredibly brief and to the point.*

7. *The centurion said he did not deserve to have Jesus come into his home. He knew Jesus could heal the servant with just a word. The centurion was a man of authority, and he recognized Jesus as a man of authority as well. Jesus described the centurion's faith as unmatched in all of Israel.*

8. *Answers will vary. One way to grow in your faith is to simply ask God for its increase. He is faithful to answer that prayer. Another way for increased faith is to faithfully pray for things only God can do. Ask God what He wants to do in your life and make a list of seemingly impossible things you'd like to ask God to do. Pray consistently. Remain patient and watch for what God may want to do!*

Digging Deeper

The verbs that should be circled are: *trust, do, dwell, enjoy, delight, commit, trust* (**again**) *be, wait, refrain,* and *turn.* Answers will vary, but it can be difficult to place all your trust in God, but easy to delight in God. Some participants may find it easy to commit to God, but harder to dwell in Him.

Chapter 8: Tapping into His Power

Focus: *Apart from God, we can do nothing.*
God is the one who is the source of everything.
To become all God wants us to be, we
need to remain "plugged in" to Him.

1. *Answers will vary, but may include: cell phones, computers, curling irons, refrigerators, microwaves, irons, stoves, dishwashers, power tools, and other devices.*

2. *Edison definitely had a natural curiosity and, to some extent, he had to rely on his imagination in order to see things that didn't yet exist. On some level, most people enjoy creating, inventing, or finding solutions because of the satisfaction.*

3. *Jeremiah 32:17 says, "Ah, Sovereign Lord, you have made the heavens and the earth by your great power and outstretched arm. Nothing is too hard for you." It's important to remember this truth about God before we begin to pray because it reminds us that God can do anything. Nothing is beyond His power. Nothing is beyond His grasp. Remembering this builds our faith and increases our ability to trust God.*

4. *Answers will vary, but the psalm is a reminder of God's power, goodness, faithfulness, love, and the great lengths to which He will go on our behalf.*

5. *Answers*

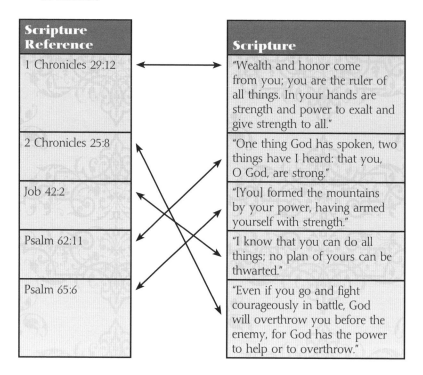

Scripture Reference	Scripture
1 Chronicles 29:12	"Wealth and honor come from you; you are the ruler of all things. In your hands are strength and power to exalt and give strength to all."
2 Chronicles 25:8	"One thing God has spoken, two things have I heard: that you, O God, are strong."
Job 42:2	"[You] formed the mountains by your power, having armed yourself with strength."
Psalm 62:11	"I know that you can do all things; no plan of yours can be thwarted."
Psalm 65:6	"Even if you go and fight courageously in battle, God will overthrow you before the enemy, for God has the power to help or to overthrow."

6. *Answers will vary.*

7. *Answers will vary, but stress, exhaustion, and business can all distract us from the truth of who God is and the power He has in our lives.*

8. *Answers will vary, but encourage participants to commit to various spiritual disciplines including: prayer, study, fasting, and solitude.*

Digging Deeper

Jesus is the "true vine." God is the "gardener." Answers will vary, but Jesus is the way to eternal life and God is the Creator of our universe.

Chapter 9: Stories of Great Faith

Focus: *Whether you realize it or not, you have a great story of faith. While it may not be as dramatic as some, your story is unique and God wants you to use it to share the good news of who He is and all that He has done.*

1. *Encourage each participant to share, in two minutes or less, their conversion experience. If the participant seems to be running longer than desired, gently remind her to keep it brief. Don't make anyone feel forced to share; some may be uncomfortable in sharing. Take note of all the ways God uses us to draw people closer to Himself.*

2. *Answers will vary. Some people will feel more comfortable than others in sharing their stories of meeting God. Encourage participants who may be shy about sharing. They may feel their stories are not as meaningful as others'. Assure them that every story matters.*

3. *Answers will vary. In general, all participants' lives have been changed by God and continue to be changed by Him—perhaps by this very Bible study.*

4. *The angel instructed Philip to go to a specific place on a road. Only after he obeyed this direction did the Spirit speak to him again, telling him to go to a specific chariot and stay near it.*

5. *Answers will vary, but it's incredible to think of all the specific things God's Spirit will lead us to do, including: giving things away, sharing our faith, and encouraging others.*

6. *Philip began by looking for an opportunity to help the eunuch understand the Scriptures. Then he accepted the invitation from the eunuch to spend time with him in his chariot. Philip explained a specific passage the eunuch was curious about and proceeded to share the good news about Jesus. Finally, Philip baptized the eunuch as he requested.*

7. *The principles demonstrated in this passage include being obedient and responsive to God's leading in your life. Also demonstrated is the importance of building relational bridges with others. Only in relationship can we discover the needs and spiritual questions others may have. This passage illustrates the importance of knowing the Scriptures and being able to share the good news. It also reveals the power of God to change someone's heart.*

8. *Answers will vary, but as followers of God, the good news we have is simply too good to keep to ourselves. Jesus instructed His disciples to go to the ends of the earth to make followers of God (Matthew 28:19–20). Most of us have only to go a few houses down from our own to find people who don't yet know Jesus.*

Digging Deeper

Meditating on God's Word is the primary way of getting to know God. Through the Scriptures, we discover who God is and what a healthy relationship with Him looks like. If we don't personally study and meditate on God's Word, we will be forced to rely on what others say about God instead of knowing Him for ourselves.

Chapter 10: Nothing Is Impossible for God

Focus: *Faith invites us to step beyond ourselves and truly believe in God with our whole selves. Through faith, we have the opportunity to watch the God of the universe do the impossible in our lives, as well as in the lives of those we love.*

1. *Answers will vary, but we've all been in situations in which we've needed to depend on God. Like the man in this story, we are sometimes tempted to look for another option instead of trusting in God.*

2. *Faith isn't easy. Often, we try to handle things on our own. We may prefer to trust what is familiar or known rather than turning to an invisible yet all-powerful and all-knowing God.*

3. *Some people find it easier to trust God than others. This can be based on a variety of reasons, including personal experience, past history, and knowledge of God. Yet, choosing to trust God (whether or not it comes easily for you in some situations) tends to stir up fears, doubts, and issues of belief in God's love.*

4. *This was a homecoming for Jesus. He was returning to His hometown. The people responded to Jesus with amazement, wonder, and quite a few questions. They wanted to know where He got His wisdom; if He was really the carpenter's son; and if He was still the Jesus they had known years before.*

5. *Jesus didn't perform many miracles because of the people's lack of faith. While the Bible doesn't say Jesus would have performed more miracles had the situation been different, the passage implies the lack of faith was the key issue. One could speculate, since this was Jesus' hometown, He would naturally have wanted to share God's power, including healing and restoration, with those He knew and grew up with.*

6. *Hebrews 11:6 says, "And without faith it is impossible to please God, because anyone who comes to him must believe that he exists and that he rewards those who earnestly seek him." Answers will vary as to why faith is so pleasing to God. However, through faith we express our dependence on God and acknowledge that He truly is who He says He is.*

7. *James said we must believe and not doubt when we pray. Doubt will lead to a person's being confused and tossed about. Answers will vary regarding prayer without faith.*

8. *Answers will vary, but sometimes we need to jump-start our prayer lives by asking God to do the impossible in an area of our lives.*

Digging Deeper

Elisha asked the woman to collect all the jars in her neighborhood and fill them with oil. The woman did what she was told and ended up with enough oil to pay off her debts and an abundance she and her son could live on. Answers will vary. Even though we might not have experienced a miracle as this woman did, God can still do wonders through those who are faithful and obedient.

Chapter 11: Believing in the Impossible

Focus: *What God is doing in our lives is impossible to imagine. By stepping out in our faith, we can risk knowing and believing Jesus as our Savior.*

1. Peter said, "Lord, if it's you, tell me to come to you on the water" (Matthew 14:28). He wanted to confirm whether or not what he was seeing was really Jesus.

2. Faith played a huge role in this story. Without faith, Peter would never have stepped out of the boat. All of the disciples' faith was strengthened by what they saw and experienced.

3. Answers will vary. Some may interpret Jesus' tone as firm or frustrated.

4. Jesus asked the Samaritan woman for a drink of water. According to verse 9, the Samaritan woman was surprised. She knew Jews and Samaritans did not usually associate.

5. Jesus answered her, "If you knew the gift of God and who it is that asks you for a drink, you would have asked him and he would have given you living water" (John 4:10).

6. Jesus asked the woman to call her husband. The woman admitted that she did not have a husband—the truth, but not the whole truth. The woman had known five husbands and was not married to the man with whom she was currently living.

7. *Jesus revealed that He is the Messiah. The woman responded by leaving her water jar at the well and running to tell the people in her city about Jesus. She became an evangelist, telling the Samaritans the good news of Jesus.*

8. *Answers will vary. Invite participants to share what risks they are planning to take.*

Digging Deeper

Jesus' ability to walk on water identified Him as the Son of God. God has complete power over nature and nothing is impossible for Him.

Chapter 12: Called to the Impossible

Focus: *As you seek God and grow in your relationship with Him, you will find yourself growing in faith. You'll discover God wants to do more than you ever imagined; not because of anything you do, but simply because of who He is.*

1. *Answers will vary. Many will be surprised that Colson went from being a prisoner to saving the lost. Others will be surprised that he was once involved with Watergate and went on to create an amazingly successful prison outreach program.*

2. *Answers will vary, but may include words like:* steady, fruitful, abounding, silent, scarce, painful, difficult, challenging, joyful, delightful, simple, complex, or repetitive. *Encourage participants to honestly share what they're feeling.*

3. *Answers will vary, but may include:* celebratory, consistent, joyful, productive, easy, or comfortable. *Gently remind participants that prayer is a spiritual discipline—it takes practice and consistency. Prayer becomes more natural the more we do it. And we serve a God who wants to hear from us all day, every day.*

4. *Answers will vary but may include* honest, focused, genuine, humble, *and* consistent.

5. *The Scriptures say the man will get up and provide bread because of his boldness. The story suggests prayer is essential. We should not hold back, but should ask God for what we need and desire.*

6. *Answers will vary. Hopefully, this interpretation will help readers see this passage in a new light and reflect on the character of God.*

7. *Answers will vary. Hopefully, this realization will provide great comfort and increased faith in our God who answers prayer, based not on us, but based on who He is.*

8. *Answers will vary, but encourage the women to share one rich lesson received from this study.*

Digging Deeper

Answers will vary. Many participants may turn to a spouse, friend, prayer, or their Bible when they are anxious. In this verse, we are asked to turn to God in prayer. Everyone will have their own stories to share on how prayer has affected their lives.

Notes

Chapter 1: Embrace Your Imagination

1. *Dictionary.com*, s.v. "imagine." http://dictionary.reference.com/browse/imagine (accessed September 11, 2009).

Chapter 9: Stories of Great Faith

1. Percy Parker, ed., *The Journal of John Wesley* (Chicago: Moody Press, 1951).

2. Ibid.

Chapter 10: Nothing Is Impossible for God

1. *Sermon Illustrations*, s.v. "Faith," http://www.sermonillustrations.com/a-z/f/faith.htm (accessed September 11, 2009).

About the Author

A popular speaker at churches and leading conferences such as Catalyst, CreationFest, and Thrive, Margaret Feinberg will spend 120 days this year on the road and speak to nearly 100,000 people. Recently named by *Charisma* magazine one of the "30 Emerging Voices" who will help lead the church in the next decade, she has written more than two dozen books and Bible studies, including the critically acclaimed *The Organic God, The Sacred Echo, Scouting the Divine,* and their corresponding DVD Bible studies. She is known for her relational teaching style and inviting people to discover the relevance of God and His Word in a modern world.

Margaret and her books have been covered by national media, including CNN, the Associated Press, *Los Angeles Times, Dallas Morning News, Washington Post, Chicago Tribune,* and many others. She currently lives in Morrison, Colorado, with her 6'8" husband, Leif. Go ahead, become her friend on Facebook, follow her on twitter @ mafeinberg, or check out her website at www.margaretfeinberg.com.

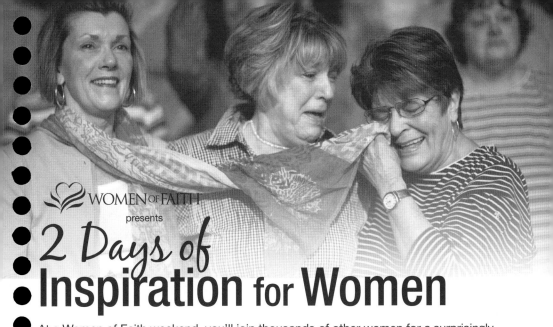

WOMEN OF FAITH

presents

Two Tours. 29 Cities.
Countless Lives Changed.

Join us at one of these life-changing events!
See when we'll be in your area. Go to **womenoffaith.com** for current
schedule and talent lineup.

Imagine Coming to:

Billings, MT	**Denver, CO**
April 9–10, 2010	September 24–25, 2010
Las Vegas, NV	**Phoenix, AZ**
April 23–24, 2010	October 1–2, 2010
Omaha, NE	**Portland, OR**
August 13–14, 2010	October 8–9, 2010
Dallas, TX	**San Antonio, TX**
August 20–21, 2010	October 22–23, 2010
Tulsa, OK	**Seattle, WA**
August 27–28, 2010	October 29–30, 2010
Anaheim, CA	**Kansas City, MO**
September 10–11, 2010	November 5–6, 2010
Spokane, WA	**Sacramento, CA**
September 17–18, 2010	November 12–13, 2010

Over the Top Coming to:

Des Moines, IA	**Milwaukee, WI**
March 12–13, 2010	October 1–2, 2010
Shreveport, LA	**Rochester, NY**
April 23–24, 2010	October 8–9, 2010
Columbus, OH	**Tampa, FL**
April 30–May 1	October 15–16, 2010
Indianapolis, IN	**St. Paul, MN**
August 20–21, 2010	October 22–23, 2010
Washington DC	**Ft. Lauderdale, FL**
August 27–28, 2010	November 5–6, 2010
Philadelphia, PA	**Greensboro, NC**
September 10–11, 2010	November 12–13, 2010
Cleveland, OH	**Hartford, CT**
September 17–18, 2010	November 19–20, 2010
Atlanta (Duluth), GA	
September 24–25, 2010	

Imagine and *Over the Top* are productions of Thomas Nelson Live Events. Date, location, and talent subject to change.